1-30-75

BORDER PATROL

How U.S. Agents Protect
Our Borders from Illegal Entry

1974 Marked the 50th Anniversary of the Border Patrol

by C.B. COLBY

Coward, McCann & Geoghegan, Inc.
New York

**YUMA STATION 1927
UNITED STATES BORDER PATROL**

Contents

Photo Credit

All photos, including the two full-color cover transparencies, were supplied through the courtesy of the United States Border Patrol of the Immigration and Naturalization Service of the United States Department of Justice. All are official Border Patrol photographs.

© 1974 by C.B. Colby   All rights reserved   Printed in the United States of America

SBN: GB-698-30542-6

SBN: TR-698-20290-2

Library of Congress Catalog Card Number: 73-88536

The Border Patrol Story

The United States of America is one of the few countries in the world with unguarded borders. Lured by the promise of freedom and the hope of prosperity, many citizens of other countries may make illegal, often desperate attempts to cross our borders, hoping to begin a new life here. It is these people who are the targets of the United States Border Patrol, the law enforcement branch of the Immigration and Naturalization Service of the United States Department of Justice.

During a recent year approximately 503,896 people, of whom 498,123 were found to be deportable aliens, were apprehended by Border Patrol agents. This group included 6,355 smugglers who attempted to bring a total of 41,589 aliens into the country illegally. Also in this group were 3,342 violators of other laws including 1,984 narcotics violators. The value of the contraband seized and stolen property recovered in that same year amounted to more than $21,000,000.

The Border Patrol was begun in 1924 with 450 officers who were hastily recruited, poorly trained, and shabbily equipped. As you can see from the 1927 photo on the opposite page, they did not even have uniforms. Today the force numbers approximately 1,700 splendidly trained, well-equipped, and smartly uniformed officers.

The "beat" of these officers is divided into three sectors. The northern border of the United States which we share with Canada is one sector. Known as the longest undefended border in the world, it stretches 3,987 miles from Point Roberts, Washington, to Calais, Maine. The second sector is the Mexican/United States border, running 1,945 miles from San Ysidro, California, eastward to Port Isabel, Texas. Much of this boundary runs down the middle of the Rio Grande. The third sector runs along the Gulf Coast and up the east coast of Florida to Georgia, for another 2,057 miles. This makes a total of about 8,000 miles that are under the watchful eyes and ears of the Border Patrol.

The infiltration of aliens from Canada across our northern border is minimal since legal entry is simple and the economies of the two countries are so similar. Still, some of the sea borders do present problems because of the commercial and private shipping. Smuggling by boats is not uncommon and must be counteracted by the Border Patrol.

It is along the Mexican/United States boundary that the patrol meets its greatest challenge. For many poor people from Mexico and other South and Central American countries it represents a 1,945-mile-long gateway to the United States and a hoped-for solution to their problems. Since much of this border is unfenced and seems to be unguarded, it appears simple to slip across. Attempts to wade across the shallow Rio Grande have for years been common. The soaking wet would-be Americans came to be known as wetbacks. Professional smugglers offer aliens all sorts of propositions for smuggling them over the border. Their fees are usually high, and the chance of success is low.

To help guard against this year-around invasion of illegal aliens, the Border Patrol, whose official assignment by law is "to detect and prevent the smuggling and unlawful entry of Aliens into the United States," has developed sophisticated equipment and methods to detect and apprehend illegal border crossers.

In this book you will learn about the training of Border Patrol agents, what types of checking they do to find aliens, how they spot aliens attempting to cross or already over the border, and what tricks the smugglers use to try to slip aliens through our thousands of miles of open boundary.

I would like to express my appreciation to Robert L. Stewart and Robin J. Clack, veteran Border Patrol agents and assistants to the Deputy Associate Commissioner, Domestic Control, and to Donald R. Coppock, Deputy Associate Commissioner, Domestic Control. To them, many thanks for their cooperation in making this book such an interesting project.

C. B. COLBY

Where Border Patrol Training Begins

The Border Patrol Academy, where patrol agents are trained, is located at Los Fresnos, Texas, about as far south as you can go in Texas, near Brownsville. Here the trainees undergo a fourteen-week course of instruction in every phase of immigration law enforcement and basic preparation for a career in the patrol. Above is a view of the modern academy, and on the opposite page (top to bottom) is a view of a typical student lounge in a trainee dormitory and one of trainees studying Spanish and becoming experts in first aid. The program of study includes such things as training in fluent Spanish, immigration law, court procedure, constitutional rights, interrogation, "sign cutting" (tracking), and aerial observation. The trainees also learn to use electronic surveillance equipment, radios, firearms, and many other modern-day tools of the Border Patrol.

4

Learning Tricks of the Trade

The trainee patrol agents must learn all the "trade secrets" of the law enforcement officer, as well as those of criminals or would-be aliens they might encounter. Above, a class learns all about the various weapons an alien might be carrying, from authentic firearms to homemade zip guns, ice picks, brass knuckles, and farm tools converted into deadly weapons. Even chains, vehicle ornaments, and belt and harness buckles can be potential killers when used by a desperate man. The opposite page (top) shows instruction in fingerprinting and (below) an agent learning to interrogate a suspect. In some cases undercover agents of the patrol (who know almost all the tricks of a suspect by heart) play the suspect. Everything possible is done to prepare the future agents for the exacting and often dangerous work of guarding our country's borders.

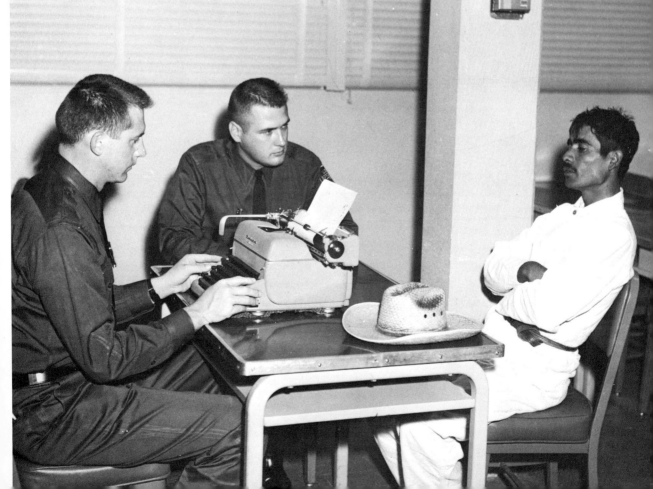

Physical Training, Too

Not only must the Border Patrol Agent be alert and superbly trained to detect illegal aliens, but he must be in top physical condition in order to protect himself when apprehending a suspect. Above, we see trainees being timed over a "confidence course" (top) and (lower) developing powerful wrists and hands by winding up heavy weights attached to stout cords. On the opposite page we see an instructor (left) demonstrating how to handle an uncooperative border-crossing suspect. Often an aggressive approach by the agent saves more serious injury to both agent and suspect. All Border Patrol agents are experts with all types of firearms and must requalify four times a year to keep up their high standards of marksmanship. The patrol pistol team has won almost every championship trophy it has competed for.

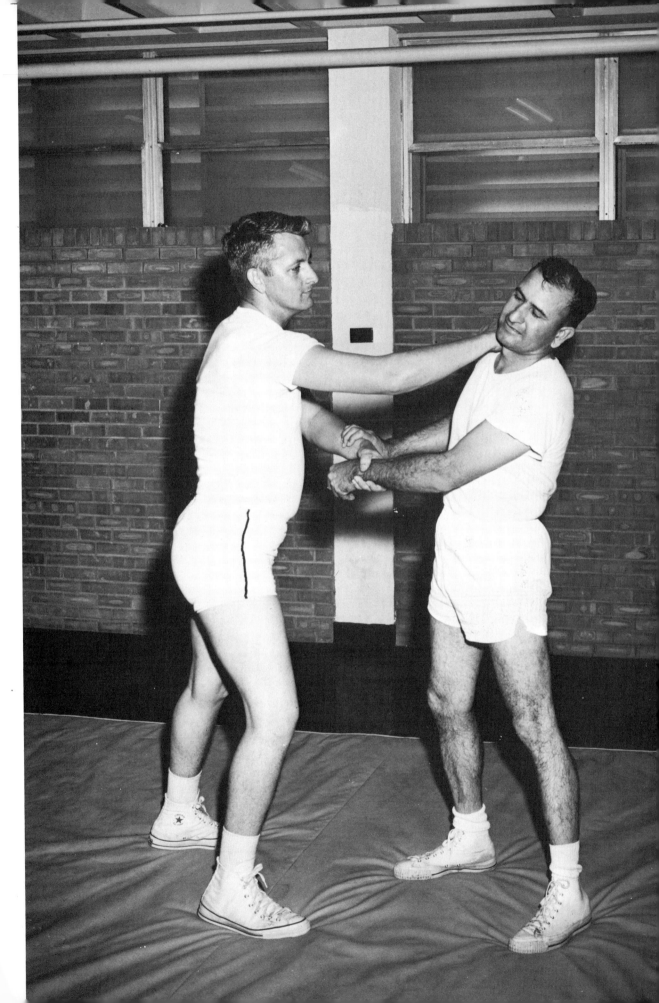

Our "Undefended" Border

Although mention of the United States Border Patrol invariably reminds one of the U.S. Mexican border, cactus and "wetbacks" crossing the Rio Grande, the patrol also helps protect the 3,987 miles of the U.S./Canadian border as well. Often called the longest undefended international boundry, this border, stretching from Point Roberts Washington, to Calais, Maine, presents many problems never encountered in the south. Above, a mounted Border Patrol unit scouts the rugged mountains of our Northwest, and opposite we see various agents in a canoe, on snowshoes, working from a boat, and checking cars on a trailer train for hidden aliens. Since the economy of Canada is so close to that of the United States, the flow of aliens across the border from Canada is far less than from Mexico. Here, too, border crossing restrictions are less strict. Still, the countersmuggling program must be extensive, and the patrol must be equipped for both winter and summer operations.

Border Show and Tell

A person near the U.S./Canadian border never knows when he will encounter an agent of the Border Patrol. He may be asked to show some identification and tell what his business or destination is. Above, we see some ice fishermen on a boundary line lake being checked, and some young hitchhikers being questioned. Whether on a main highway close to the border or deep in the wilderness, the Border Patrol agents are ever alert for signs of possible illegal entry. They use every means of transportation and communication to keep up with the tricks of would-be border crossers. The opposite page shows a patrol agent with his own snowmobile checking the credentials of another snowmobiler close to the border, and another agent checks the identification of the operator of a tracked over-snow vehicle working near a portion of the boundary. Although deep snow makes transportation more difficult, it also makes tracking of border jumpers easier.

Waterfront Checkup

With so many lakes, rivers, and ponds straddling or serving as a portion of the U.S./Canadian border, patrol agents must be familiar with every inch of these waterways and every trick of aliens who might want to cross into the United States via water. Above, an agent of the Border Patrol probes a cargo of raw hides aboard a ship entering the port of Buffalo, New York. Would-be aliens will try many ways to enter the United States. Some will even hide amid a pile of bloody and strong-smelling animal hides for days at a stretch to enter our country. The opposite page shows a patrol agent checking the papers of a fishing boat working international waters in Blaine, Washington. The use of high-speed boats is popular with those who try to smuggle aliens across the water boundary.

Aliens Can Be Anywhere

Although the U.S./Canadian border is easy to cross legally with proper credentials, those who fear a confrontation with the law prefer to try to slip into the United States and avoid any contact with the authorities. This is not as easy as many like to think, and there are few places an alien can hide from veteran Border Patrol agents. Above, we see an agent checking the credentials of a young groom from Canada at the Buffalo Raceway in Hamburg, New York. These Border Patrol officers are officially known as patrol agents. The opposite page shows these agents checking a junkyard and maple sugar workers gathering sap near the border in New York and (bottom) searching an illegal entrant on the shore of Rainy Lake, North Dakota. The patrolling of the U.S./Mexican border presents a completely different picture, as the following pages will reveal.

The Border Patrol Is Watching

The U.S./Mexican border stretches for 1,945 miles from San Ysidro, California, to the Gulf of Mexico. It crosses mountains, deserts, and canyons and passes through rich farmlands. It divides towns and villages and runs down the center of the famed Rio Grande. It is marked by high fences near civilization and by simple concrete markers in uninhabited wilderness areas. Its entire length, fenced or wide open, is patrolled in one way or another. In the above photo a Border Patrol agent watches an unsuspecting alien (on the road, near the railroad tracks in the center of the photo) who has just crossed through the opening in the fence where the tracks cross into the United States. On the opposite page, another officer keeps an eye on another unsuspecting alien crossing a wilderness stretch of border. This alien can be seen at top of path up the slope at the right. He is carrying a large white bag of belongings or contraband over his shoulder. Both these aliens were later apprehended.

Drag Strips Help Trap Aliens

To make detection of aliens crossing the Mexican border easier, the Border Patrol has developed some ingenious tricks. One of them is the drag strip, not used in this case for racing high-speed cars, but for the detection of footprints and other signs of aliens crossing the boundary. Above, we see two devices used for making these drag strips. The area along the American side of the boundary is cleared of all brush and rocks, and then the dirt is smoothed by dragging various devices over it. These include wheeled units (top) and towed screens (lower) to smooth the area. On the opposite page are shown (top and center) footprints of aliens who entered illegally. The bottom photo shows the apprehension of an illegal entrant who was tracked into the desert. Border Patrol agents are expert trackers over all kinds of terrain by day or night.

Towers and Train Check

Where the drag strip runs in a fairly straight line and alien traffic is expected to be heavy, tall towers linked by phone or radio help the patrol keep watch for illegal crossings. Checking border-crossing traffic and trains often turns up illegal aliens who slip by undetected. Above is a traffic van at a border-crossing spot on a highway. Blinking lights and the stop-sign signal traffic to stop for a Border Patrol check. If a car tries to run the roadblock, a message is radioed ahead to set up a roadblock further on to catch the suspect. Lights are run from a generator in the van which also contains a wide variety of equipment, such as floodlights to assist in detecting hidden contraband. The opposite page shows a surveillance tower on a border drag strip and (lower) patrol agents boarding a freight train to look for aliens.

Air and Underground Surveillance

A fleet of twenty-two single-engine aircraft help patrol our borders and assist in checking field workers (above) some of whom may be illegal aliens. Helicopters, although they have been used in some instances, are generally too short-ranged for patrol over long periods. The small planes are ideal for working with ground units and lone agents working on special assignments. Another underground assist is literally under the ground. These are small vibration sensors hidden along the border at strategic spots. Should anything walk over or near these tiny geophones a signal will be transmitted to either a mobile unit or a larger base station receiver. This signal will indicate on a chart or other device where an intruder is crossing. The opposite page shows (top) an agent watching a moving graph for signals from remote underground units. The lower photo shows an agent directing his partner to where the signal indicates a movement across a border. These units are so sensitive that even a very small animal or movement of roots in high winds will trigger a signal. The Border Patrol has many tricks up its uniform sleeves to nab unwanted intruders.

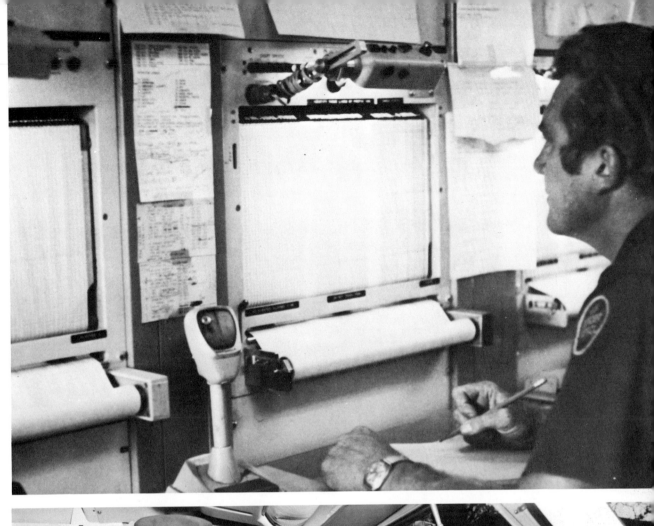

Tricks That Failed

So desperate are some aliens to enter the United States of America that they will go to dangerous lengths to cross our borders illegally. On the following pages you will see to what lengths some will go to enter the country. Often they pay hundreds of dollars to those who promise to smuggle them across the boundary. In many instances these aliens have been smothered, burned, or made desperately sick from their expensive and futile attempts to enter the United States. Above is shown a man hidden in the back of a car. He was found when the agent removed a sheet of material. On the opposite page we see two young Mexicans who tried to hide under the hood of a smuggler's car. Often this results in frightful burns from a hot engine or suffocation. Rarely do such attempts at illegal entry end successfully; and if they're not caught at the border, the fugitives are tracked down and captured for prosecution and deportation.

Amateur and Professional Carriers

The photo above shows a young boy caught while trying to slip past the patrol. He was hanging from a crude sling made of ropes and a stove grate slung under a passenger car. Border patrol agents raise suspicious cars on jacks or hydraulic lifts to inspect underneath, often finding aliens under the chassis. The opposite page shows a professional smuggler's truck equipped with two welded strap iron racks designed to carry two aliens. The top photo shows one rack empty and the other filled with a trapped intruder. The lower two photos show an unusual fiberglass "tank" under a car, which, when opened, revealed a hidden would-be border crosser. In the case of a crash none of these aliens would have had a chance of survival, but they were willing to risk it for the sake of gaining entry into the United States.

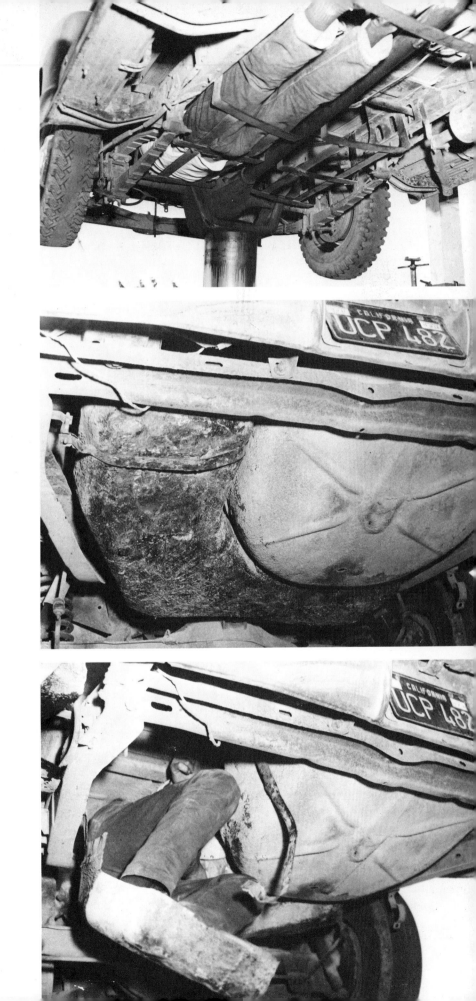

It Wasn't All Hay!

The professional alien smuggler, greedy for more profit, often goes to great lengths to smuggle in as many aliens as possible in one trip. This expensive-looking horse trailer pulled by a fine car was stopped and inspected like any battered and rusty truck. The results are shown on the opposite page. When the trailer doors were opened (top) it was discovered that the load of hay was merely a blind and that underneath was a compartment large enough to hold twenty-nine aliens who had crossed the border illegally. The lower photo shows this group of aliens caught in the attempt. The penalties for smuggling aliens are extremely severe, but there always seems to be those who think they have a trick the men of the Border Patrol haven't thought of. In almost all of these attempts they find they were wrong and pay the penalty.

Load of Junk

Only the would-be aliens who tried to sneak over the U.S./Mexican border were fooled by this trick. This harmless-looking load of junk was spotted by the Border Patrol and quickly determined to be nothing but a fake. The photo above shows how a hollow load was filled with ten aliens below the top layer. On the opposite page we see another smuggling trick that failed. The top photo opposite shows a suspicious-looking section of a truck fender and (below) what was concealed inside and under the truck floor. The danger of smothering in these cramped compartments was great, yet aliens take the risk. Hidden compartments, double floors, and many other ingenious ideas all have gone to waste when the Border Patrol goes into action to stem the flow of illegal persons across our international boundaries.

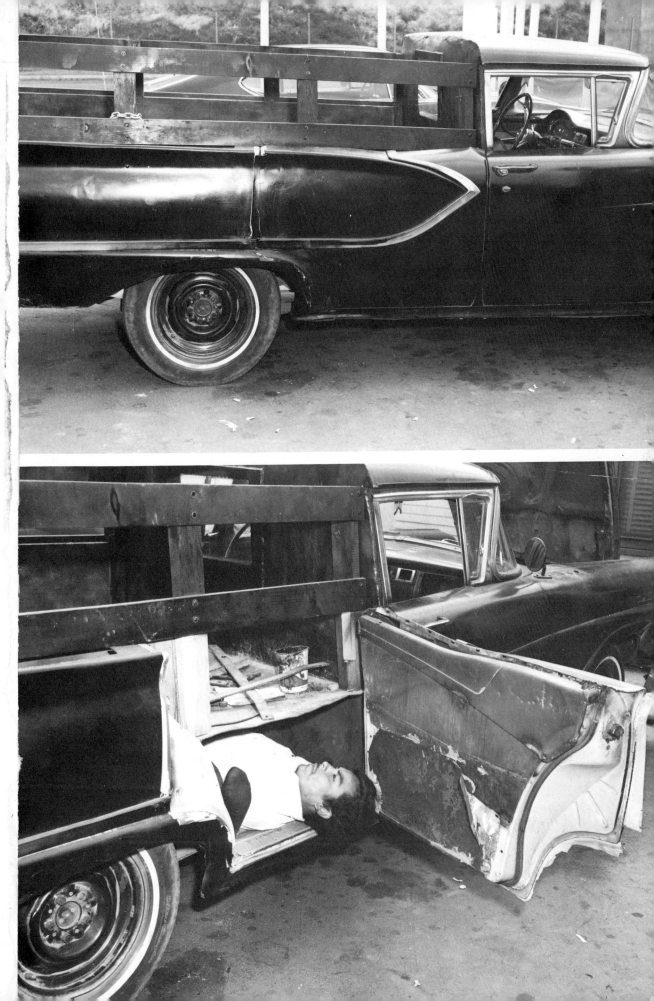

Suspicion Pays Off!

No matter how innocent a load of material crossing the American border may appear, the Border Patrol inspectors have learned to be suspicious of it. More often than not this traditional suspicion pays off. The above photo shows what happened when the agents became suspicious of a load of empty vegetable crates. Under the top layers of empty crates was a compartment containing thirty aliens who were promptly taken into custody. On the opposite page (top) is what the agents spotted when they began to check over a load of old tires being taken across the border. The lower shows the ten aliens who finally crawled out of the center of the load, as the tires were removed, another smuggling trick that failed.

1834858

Hitting the Jackpot

One of the largest groups of aliens to be apprehended while attempting to enter the United States illegally via a single vehicle is shown above. These sixty Mexicans were concealed behind a few pieces of furniture arranged to look like a full load of furniture when the rear van doors were opened. The Border Patrol was not fooled, and the aliens were quickly apprehended, along with the driver. On the opposite page (top) is another smuggling truck trick that failed. This load of empty vegetable crates had a hollow center (revealed when the outer row was removed) containing these six aliens. The lower photo shows the entrance to a secret compartment and the captured aliens.

Although the main purpose and chief assignment of the U.S. Border Patrol is to detect and to prevent the smuggling and illegal entry of aliens into the United States, its agents often discover smuggled narcotics and other illegal material during inspections of suspicious vehicles. On the next few pages you will see some of the contraband seizures made by Border Patrol agents.

Marijuana Stopped
at the Border

Above photo shows a burlap sack found near the border apparently hidden for a later pickup. It contained many one-gallon tin cans marked "Pure de Tomate." Inside, packed and sealed, were many pounds of Mexican marijuana. It never reached the illegal market. On the opposite page are photos of a tremendous haul of the illegal drugs found when a suspicious truckload of "oil drums" was examined. The top photo shows how the truck looked when stopped at the border, and the lower photos show what was found when one of the drums was opened, well-wrapped kilo bricks of marijuana, known also as pot or grass. In all, this truck carried over a ton and a half of this drug, worth a fortune on the retail market. There were twenty-one 55-gallon drums fully packed with 3,388 pounds of this illegal material which, thanks to the U.S. Broder Patrol, never reached the market.

Loads of Trouble!

It is unfortunate that there are so many people who try to smuggle both aliens or illegal materials into the United States. They should know that only a small percentage ever really profit by the attempt. The risks are tremendous and the penalties most severe for those who are caught. But still these criminally inclined persons try to beat the odds. Here are shown two "losers" who tried to smuggle marijuana across the border. The top photo shows a load of 320 kilos of marijuana, and the opposite page shows a Volkswagen fastback, carrying 280 kilos of the weed, that tried to slip by the Border Patrol along a beach. In both cases the occupants of the car were apprehended and taken into custody along with the illegal drug they carried. All along the Gulf Coast, Border Patrol agents keep an eye out for suspicious boats of all sizes and crew members who are under suspicion as possible smugglers. Agents often work from tips from undercover agents and concerned citizens. On the following pages you will see some of the Gulf Coast activity of the men of the Border Patrol.

All Size Boats Bear Watching

The Gulf coastline and the eastern coast of Florida to its northern state boundary constitutes a sea border of 2,057 miles also patrolled by the Border Patrol. There are thousands of boats of all sizes going in and out of the many ports, river mouths, and small marinas. A small percentage of these may be engaged in some type of illegal activity, either smuggling contraband, narcotics, or aliens. The boats, men, and equipment of the patrol work around the clock to find and apprehend these criminals and their cargoes. Above, a team of patrol agents check a small fishing boat and question its pilot. On the opposite page (top) a small pleasure boat and its occupants are questioned about their destination and home port and are perhaps asked if they have seen a certain suspicious boat in the area. The lower photo shows a Border Patrol agent interrogating a crew member aboard a commercial ship. Often tips on crewmen or suspicious cargoes are received from crew members, shippers, or alert passengers.

Smuggler Trouble Comes in Pairs!

Usually traveling in pairs, the men of the Border Patrol inspect thousands of ships a year along our southern sea border. The photo above shows a group of agents boarding a docked vessel to check for possible aliens or other illegal cargo. Often aliens will sneak aboard a ship completely unknown to either the crew or captain and hope to slip ashore equally undetected. In other cases a crew member, or even the captain, may arrange illegal passage, for a high price, in the hope that the alien might escape detection. The penalties for both the alien and the one who arranged the attempt are not worth the risk of detection. Photos on the opposite page show (top) two agents checking a crew member and (lower) looking over a questionable ship from the foredeck of a Border Patrol patrol boat. The seagoing officers of the patrol are well experienced in every trick of the would-be smuggler, and it takes the exceptional one to escape their keen eyes. A trick might work once, but not often twice.

Border Patrol Sector Headquarters

Many splendid headquarters buildings may be found where the U.S. Border Patrol activities are required. Here are some good examples of the modern, well-equipped, and efficient sector headquarters buildings to be found at widely separated points in the United States. Above is the Houlton Border Patrol Sector Headquarters at Houlton, Maine, as it looked during the dedication in 1965. Among those units taking part, to show their complete and important cooperation with the work of the Border Patrol, were members of the Royal Canadian Mounted Police, the Houlton Town Police, the Maine State Police, and the United States Border Patrol. Interdepartmental cooperation is important for success on both sides of the border. The opposite page shows (top to bottom) the North Dakota Sector Headquarters at Grand Forks, North Dakota; the Arizona Sector Headquarters at Tucson, Arizona; and the Border Patrol Sector Headquarters at Laredo, Texas.

Crime Fighting Fringe Benefits

Not all of the work of the Border Patrol is the grim business of tracking down aliens, smugglers, and other criminals. Since its beginning, countless acts of assistance to stranded motorists, searches for persons lost in the forests and deserts in border states, and the rescues of families trapped in floods and burning buildings by patrol agents have been reported. Patrol pilots have dropped food and medicine to villages cut off from help, and many an accident victim has been flown or driven to a hospital by the Border Patrol. In a recent hurricane emergency one officer died as a result of having worked around the clock for three days without sleep. The Border Patrol also works with youth groups. Above is shown one of the championship Little League teams sponsored and trained by members of the McAllen (Texas) Border Patrol unit. The country can be extremely proud of the United States Border Patrol, of the Immigration and Naturalization Service of the Department of Justice. No law enforcement body has a greater responsibility to America and our laws, and no other enforcement agency does a more magnificent job in the performance of its duty to America.